**J
973.7
Civil War**

Causes of the War

THE AMERICAN CIVIL WAR

★ THE RIGHT ANSWER ★

CAUSES OF THE WAR

Tim Cooke

Gareth Stevens
Publishing

Please visit our website, www.garethstevens.com. For a free color catalog of all our high-quality books, call toll free 1-800-542-2595 or fax 1-877-542-2596.

Library of Congress Cataloging-in-Publication Data
Cooke, Tim, 1961-
Causes of the war / Tim Cooke.
    p. cm. — (The American Civil War : the right answer)
Includes index.
ISBN 978-1-4339-7536-3 (pbk.)
ISBN 978-1-4339-7537-0 (6-pack)
ISBN 978-1-4339-7535-6 (library binding)
1. United States—History—Civil War, 1861-1865—Causes—Juvenile literature. 2. United States—Politics and government—1849-1861—Juvenile literature. 3. Slavery—United States—History—19th century—Juvenile literature. I. Title.
E459.C77 2013
973.7'11—dc23

                              2012004050

Published in 2013 by
Gareth Stevens Publishing
111 East 14th Street, Suite 349
New York, NY 10003

© 2013 Brown Bear Books Ltd.

For Brown Bear Books Ltd:
Editorial Director: Lindsey Lowe
Managing Editor: Tim Cooke
Children's Publisher: Anne O'Daly
Art Director: Jeni Child
Designer: Karen Perry
Picture Manager: Sophie Mortimer
Production Director: Alastair Gourlay

Picture Credits:
Front Cover: Library of Congress

Interior all Library of Congress except, National Archives: 11, 43; Robert Hunt Library: 7, 22; Thinkstock: istockphoto 37, Photos.com 5, 34, 35, 36, 42. 45.

All Artworks © Brown Bear Books Ltd.

Manufactured in the United States of America
1 2 3 4 5 6 7 8 9   12 11 10

CPSIA compliance information: Batch #BRS12GS: For further information contact Gareth Stevens, New York, New York at 1-800-542-2595.

Contents

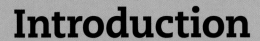

Introduction

The Civil War (1861–1865) was called "the war between brothers." It divided the United States in two. Friends took different sides and families were split apart. At the heart of the conflict lay slavery.

The Civil War that began in 1861 had many different causes. The two sides could not even agree on what they were fighting about. In the decades since the creation of the United States, the country had become highly divided.

The North and the South were different in many ways. The North had more people and more cities, while the South was more rural. The North had lots of industry, but the South had few factories. Most people there worked on farms. While Northern farms were family affairs, in the South, huge farms called plantations grew crops for export. But none of those differences alone would have led to war. There was only one thing that would have led to war between the North and the South: slavery.

About this book

This book describes the history of slavery in the United States and the main stages that led to the outbreak of the fighting. The articles are arranged in alphabetical order to make it easy to find information. Boxes in the margins help you get more out of your reading. **Comment** boxes highlight specific information and explain its importance. **Ask Yourself** boxes suggest questions for you to consider. There are no right or wrong answers; the questions are meant to help you think about the subject. Other boxes explain difficult words or ideas. The book finishes with a glossary and a list of resources for further information. There is also an index that you can use to find facts fast.

↩ *An illustration from the novel* **Uncle Tom's Cabin** *shows the death of the slave Tom. The book was so influential some peope said it helped to cause the Civil War.*

Abolition

"Abolition" was the name of a movement that aimed to end slavery in the United States. Its campaign began in the 1830s. The campaign helped make slavery an important issue in American politics.

⌒ Abolitionists use an early train to campaign for freedom for the slaves.

COMMENT

Cotton was very profitable in the 19th century. Plantation owners wanted more slaves to grow more cotton.

Many people in the Northern states spoke out against slavery as early as the American Revolution in the 1770s. But they put up with it because they knew that the Southern states would never join a union without slavery. In the South, slavery provided free labor for growing cotton and tobacco. Opponents of slavery hoped that it would just gradually die out.

Slavery had been abolished in all the states north of Maryland by 1804. Importing slaves to the United States was made illegal in 1807. But at the same time, demand for cotton grew around the world. Cotton was produced by slave labor. As more cotton was planted to meet the demand, slavery also spread.

It was clear that slavery would not gradually die out. Instead, its opponents began a movement. They called for the abolition of slavery by law.

A moral case

Historians date the beginning of the abolition movement to 1831. A Bostonian named William Lloyd Garrison began publishing *The Liberator*, a newspaper devoted to ending slavery. In 1833, he founded the American Anti-Slavery Society. Garrison and his followers believed that Christians should get rid of evils such as slavery.

Abolitionists made a moral case against slavery. They published books, magazines, and pamphlets to state their views. African Americans played a crucial role. One leading spokesman for abolition was Frederick Douglass. He was an ex-slave who wrote his autobiography in 1845. The abolitionists put moral pressure on slaveholders. In the South, many people hated the abolitionists. Many Northerners saw them as fanatics.

ASK YOURSELF

If you had lived in the North, would you care how slaves were treated in the South? Would it be any of your business?

William Lloyd Garrison was one of the leaders of the abolition movement. His Christian beliefs convinced him that slavery was immoral.

Abolitionists in Congress

Many abolitionists believed that the campaign against slavery needed political power. By the 1850s, some members of Congress were opposing legislation like the Fugitive Slave Law of 1850. The law allowed slaveowners to catch runaway slaves, even in free states. Another group were the Free Soilers. They opposed the spread of slavery for economic reasons. They formed the Free Soil Party in 1848. In 1854, they joined others to form the Republican Party, which attracted many abolitionists.

The Republican Party was founded to stop the spread of slavery. Its creation had a lasting influence on U.S. politics.

Radical action

By the 1850s, some abolitionists saw violence as the only way to solve the problem. In 1859, the abolitionist John Brown seized a federal arsenal at Harpers Ferry, Virginia. He wanted to begin a slave rebellion. Brown was quickly executed. He

⊃ *This engraving from an abolitionist publication shows a slave pleading for his freedom.*

became a symbol for abolitionists. War finally came after the election of Abraham Lincoln as president in 1860.

↻ *Wendell Phillips, a radical abolitionist, makes a speech at a rally in Boston in April 1851.*

To begin with, the abolitionists were disappointed that Lincoln did not say that he was fighting against slavery. He said that the war was to preserve the Union. But in 1863, he wrote the first version of his Emancipation Proclamation. The document made the abolition of slavery one of the Union's main aims in the war.

ASK YOURSELF

Did it matter why Lincoln said he was going to war? Wouldn't slavery have been abolished anyway if the North was victorious?

THE RIGHT ANSWER

?

How important was the abolition campaign in bringing about the end of slavery?

Union armies in the Civil War and Free Soilers in Congress probably did more to destroy slavery than the abolitionists. But the abolitionists had played an important role. Their campaign made the American public more aware of the evils of slavery. By the time war finally came, many people in the North believed that it was important to get rid of slavery. That might have made them more prepared to put up with the sacrifices and shortages of wartime. The abolitionist crusade also helped transform a war to prevent secession into a struggle for human freedom.

Causes of the Conflict

In the North, people said they were fighting the Civil War to stop the Southern states from leaving the Union. In the South, people said that they were fighting to defend their freedoms.

ASK YOURSELF

Why might the Founders have allowed slavery to exist in the United States?

The real issue, however, was slavery. Slavery had existed since colonial times. White settlers in the South bought African slaves to work on huge farms called plantations. In the early 19th century, the United States grew rapidly in the West and Southwest. But if new states were created, would they allow slavery or not? That question put slavery at the heart of politics.

In 1819, Missouri applied to join the United States as a slave state. Northern politicians worried that the South would gain too much power. They came up with the Missouri Compromise in 1820. Missouri became a slave state, but it was balanced by Maine, a new free state. Slavery was outlawed north of latitude 36° 30'. The Compromise was able to keep the peace for more than 30 years.

⊕ *This drawing shows a slave family at home.*

⊖ A slave dealer's store in Virginia, 1860. Slavery had once existed in all the North American colonies. By the time of the Civil War, it only existed in the South.

The abolition movement

There was a growing feeling in the North that slavery was wrong. That was the message of *Uncle Tom's Cabin*, published in 1852 by Harriet Beecher Stowe. The novel was a bestseller. Northerners were revolted that humans could be bought and sold like cattle. The more Northerners objected to slavery, the more Southerners defended it. They claimed slavery helped the "inferior" black race.

You can read more about *Uncle Tom's Cabin* and the woman who wrote it on page 42.

Changes in the 1850s

In 1854, the Kansas-Nebraska Act created two new territories. The settlers in each could decide whether or not to allow slavery, even though they were north of 36° 30'. The Missouri Compromise had been destroyed. Fighting in Kansas between

ASK YOURSELF

Why might white Americans have thought that black people were inferior to them?

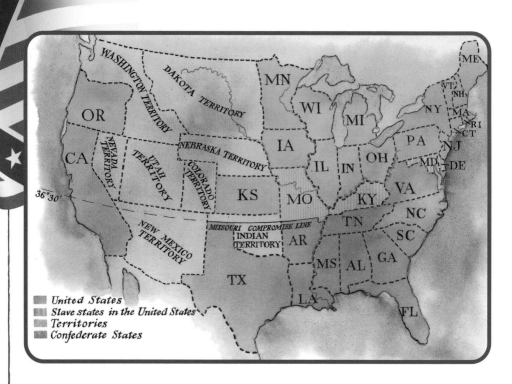

MAP LEGEND
- United States
- Slave states in the United States
- Territories
- Confederate States

This map shows which side each state took in the Civil War. Four slave states stayed in the Union: Missouri, Kentucky, Maryland, and Delaware.

supporters and opponents of slavery was so bad the period is called "Bleeding Kansas."

Late in the 1850s, tensions were increased by two events. First, in 1857, the U.S. Supreme Court ruled in the case of Dred Scott. Scott was a slave who claimed his freedom because he had lived for years in a free state and a free territory. The Court said that Scott was still a slave and that blacks could not be citizens of the United States. It also said that laws against slavery in the territories were unconstitutional. There was uproar among antislavery supporters.

In October 1859, the abolitionist John Brown led a raid on the federal arsenal at Harpers Ferry in Virginia. Brown was a fanatic. He had murdered proslavery settlers in Kansas. Now he wanted to start a slave uprising. The raid failed, and Brown was captured and hanged. In the North, he was seen as a martyr. In the South, he was no more than a murderer. Many Southerners began to think about going their separate way.

The last straw

In November 1860, the Republican Abraham Lincoln was elected president. The South was dismayed. The Republicans had campaigned to stop any spread of slavery. It seemed to many in the South that the election left them as second-class citizens. It was time to assert their rights and secede, or leave the Union.

ASK YOURSELF

Do you think John Brown should have been treated as a hero? He was a known murderer who had tried to start a rebellion against the government.

There is more about the election and its consequences on page 22.

THE RIGHT ANSWER

?

If the real cause of the Civil War was slavery, why didn't both sides just say so?

Neither side originally admitted they were fighting about slavery. In the North, President Lincoln said that he was fighting to preserve the Union. He thought that Northerners would be happier to fight for that cause than to free the slaves, which some Northerners did not really care about. In the South, people claimed they were fighting to protect the right of states to refuse laws made by the federal government. They did not say they were fighting for slavery because they wanted help from European countries that would never back a struggle for the right to own slaves.

Frederick Douglass

Frederick Douglass (c. 1818–1895) was a former slave. He spoke out against slavery and became a famous abolitionist. His autobiography described slave life as it really was.

⌒ *Frederick Douglass became a leader of the abolition campaign. He was famed for his skill at public speaking.*

F rederick Douglass was born to a slave mother in rural Maryland in 1817 or 1818. A slave's son automatically became a slave. Frederick's father was white, but Frederick never knew anything about him. The baby was originally named Frederick Augustus Washington Bailey.

At age eight, Frederick was separated from his mother. He was sent to Baltimore to be a slave in the home of Hugh and Sophia Auld. Mrs. Auld began teaching the boy to read and write. When Hugh Auld found out, he stopped her. People thought that if slaves could read and write, they would encourage each other to revolt. But Douglass had already learned enough to be able to teach himself. In his later life, he became famous for expressing himself very well in his writing. He was also a famous public speaker.

Douglass remained in Baltimore as a house slave for seven years. Then he became a plantation slave again. The conditions were brutal. After six years, he escaped to the North and settled in Massachusetts. To help escape slave hunters, he changed his name to Douglass.

In 1841, Douglass spoke at an antislavery meeting, where he described his life as a slave. His account moved his listeners. With the help of leading abolitionists, Douglass began giving lectures for the Massachusetts Anti-Slavery Society. In 1845, Douglass published his autobiography and became even more famous. Three years later, he even went to Great Britain to

House slaves often enjoyed better conditions than slaves who worked in the fields.

COMMENT

For many whites, a speaker such as Douglass might be the only real chance to find out about life as a slave.

↩ *This modern mural on the side of a building in Washington, D.C., celebrates Douglass's life.*

lecture against slavery. He earned enough money to buy his freedom and to start an antislavery newspaper. He was one of the leading abolitionists campaigning against slavery.

Political campaigner

Douglass believed that it would take more than moral argument to end slavery. He thought it needed political action, too, or even violence. In 1850, Congress passed the Fugitive Slave Act. It allowed escaped slaves to be caught, even in free

⟳ *This 1943 painting shows Douglass (right) with President Lincoln (seated).*

states. Douglass seemed to suggest that slave hunters should be killed. He also began to use a menacing catchphrase: "Who would be free must himself strike the first blow!"

In 1860, Douglass supported Abraham Lincoln's presidential campaign. When the Republicans won, Douglass saw a chance to end slavery. He served as an advisor to Lincoln throughout the Civil War. He recruited black soldiers to serve in the Union armies. Two of his own sons fought in the 54th Massachusetts regiment.

After the war, Douglass continued to campaign for full civil rights for African Americans until his death in 1895.

ASK YOURSELF

Is it ever justified to use violence to overcome an evil such as slavery? Or is violence always wrong?

Today, Douglass is seen as one of the earliest leaders of the civil rights movement.

THE RIGHT ANSWER

?

What influence did Frederick Douglass have on the campaign to abolish slavery?

No one individual brought about the abolition of slavery, but Douglass played a key role. His skill with words allowed him to express the real misery of being a slave. He also showed up the Southern claim that blacks were inferior people who were not capable of thinking like whites. Douglass was a figurehead of the abolition movement. He was the most famous African American of his time. His example helped make whites more determined to get rid of slavery. In the end, however, it was battles rather than arguments that brought freedom for the slaves.

Dred Scott Case

In March 1857, the U.S. Supreme Court made one of the most significant legal decisions in history. Its ruling about a runaway slave, Dred Scott, led to rising tensions between free and slave states.

In 1833, Dred Scott had been bought as a slave by Missouri physician John Emerson. Emerson moved around for work. He took Scott to live in Illinois, a free state, and in Wisconsin Territory, where slavery was also banned. After nine years, they returned to Missouri.

Scott sues for his freedom

Emerson died in 1843. Three years later, Scott and his wife, Harriet, went to the Missouri state court to claim their freedom from Emerson's widow.

↻ *Dred Scott lived as a slave in free territory for nine years.*

Scott said that he was entitled to his freedom because he had lived in free territory. In 1852, the Missouri Supreme Court ruled against Scott. It said that federal laws about slavery did not apply within Missouri. The ruling was upheld by a federal trial court in Missouri. Scott then appealed to the U.S. Supreme Court.

⊖ *This extract from a newspaper announces a book about the Dred Scott case. No other case in Supreme Court history has caused such an uproar.*

Supreme Court ruling

The Supreme Court decided against Scott in March 1857. All nine justices of the court issued separate opinions, which explained their decision. Seven justices backed the judgment of the trial court, so Scott had clearly lost his case.

The lead opinion was written by the Chief Justice, Roger B. Taney. Taney argued that African Americans were not citizens of the United States, so they had no right to bring cases in the federal courts. Taney also said that Scott's argument that he had lived in the free territory of Wisconsin

ASK YOURSELF

If African Americans were not citizens of the United States, what was their legal status in the country?

⤷ This magazine front page shows Scott and his wife, Harriet.

Today, most legal experts think that Taney was wrong in his interpretation of the Constitution.

was not valid. Slavery was banned in Wisconsin Territory by the terms of the 1820 Missouri Compromise. But Taney ruled that the ban on slavery was against the U.S. Constitution.

Reaction to the ruling

The ruling caused uproar in the North. Taney's view that black people had no rights was a clear victory for slavery. His ruling on the Missouri Compromise was also controversial. Only once before had the Supreme Court said that an act of Congress was unlawful. If Congress did not have the power to outlaw slavery, did the federal government have the power to force laws on individual states?

The Dred Scott decision was a big step on the path to Civil War. It showed that the Constitution could block federal efforts to stop slavery in the new territories. But blocking the spread of slavery was the central goal of the new Republican Party. Republicans began to see the Constitution as part of the problem. When the Republican Abraham Lincoln ran for president in 1860, he argued that the Constitution would have to change.

> The Constitution allowed the Supreme Court to rule on whether acts of Congress were legal or not.

> **ASK YOURSELF**
>
> Why might people be reluctant to change the Constitution?

THE RIGHT ANSWER

?

What were the main effects of the Supreme Court ruling in the Dred Scott case?

The Supreme Court decision left Scott a slave. It also made it almost impossible for the Republican Party to achieve its aim of limiting the spread of slavery. But Scott was finally freed by his owner in May 1857. And instead of undermining the Republican Party, the decision led to increased support for their antislavery ideas. This added to the tensions that led to war in 1861. The most serious victim of the case was the authority of the Court itself. The Dred Scott decision became a lasting symbol of judges acting out of personal prejudice, rather than applying the law.

Election of 1860

The election of 1860 was bitterly fought. The Democratic Party was split, and the Republicans won the election. When Abraham Lincoln became president, the South left the Union.

⌐ *Abraham Lincoln is inaugurated as president in Washington, D.C., in March 1861.*

The Republican Party had only been formed in 1854. Their policies appealed to people in the Northeast and the West. Above all, the party was opposed to any further territorial expansion of slavery. Lincoln was a natural choice for a presidential candidate. He had spoken out against slavery and had few enemies. His running mate was Hannibal Hamlin of Maine.

The Democratic Party was strained. Southern Democrats wanted to protect slavery, while Northern Democrats did not. The party split into two opposed groups. They each nominated their own candidate for the election.

There was no real opposition to Lincoln. Some veteran politicians formed the Constitutional Union Party. It wanted to create a compromise over slavery. The press called it the "soothing syrup" party. But by now, many Southerners saw defeat as inevitable. If Lincoln and his so-called "Black Republicans" won, Southerns threatened that their states would leave the Union.

Election results

The election was held on November 6, 1860. Lincoln only got 39.8 percent of the popular vote. The Northern Democrat, Stephen Douglas, got 29.5 percent. But in the electoral college, Lincoln got 180 votes; Douglas only got 12 votes. The Southern Democrat, John C. Breckinridge, was third in the popular vote, but second in the electoral college. Abraham Lincoln would become the 16th president of the United States.

The term "Black Republicans" was used by Democrats to suggest that the Republicans supported African Americans.

ASK YOURSELF

If Lincoln had not won such a big majority in the electoral college, would he still have had the confidence to go to war?

THE RIGHT ANSWER

?

Did Abraham Lincoln's victory in the 1860 election mean that civil war was inevitable?

Abraham Lincoln was elected by a minority of the people. But Stephen Douglas also opposed the expansion of slavery. Their combined total meant that 69.3 percent of voters supported that view. Candidates in favor of expanding slavery got only 30.7 percent of the vote. The South feared that Lincoln would use the result to act against slavery. On December 17, 1860, South Carolina held a secession convention. The delegates voted 169 to 0 to take the state out of the Union. Six more states followed. Lincoln was determined to keep the Union together. War was inevitable.

Kansas-Nebraska Act

The Kansas-Nebraska Act came into force in 1854. It said that settlers in new U.S. territory could decide for themselves whether to permit slavery. The act enraged opponents of slavery.

In 1853, Senator Stephen A. Douglas introduced a bill in Congress. He wanted to create a new territory of the United States, Nebraska.

Douglas came from Chicago, Illinois. He hoped to encourage the building of a transcontinental railroad that would pass through Nebraska on its way from Chicago to California. Congressmen from the South blocked the bill. They wanted a transcontinental railroad to follow a more southern route that would benefit the South.

In order to get support from the South, Douglas revised his bill. Now it would create two

➲ This is a political cartoon from 1854. It shows Liberty, "the fair maid of Kansas," being mistreated. It is a criticism of the violence in "Bleeding Kansas."

LIBERTY, THE FAIR MAID OF KANSAS—IN THE HANDS OF THE "BORDER RUFFIANS"

new territories, Nebraska and Kansas. The bill introduced what Douglas called "popular sovereignty." That meant that settlers would be allowed to vote on whether their new territory would or would not allow slavery. It was likely that Nebraska would vote against slavery. Kansas, however, was next to the slaveholding state of Missouri. Many people thought that Kansans would vote to allow slavery.

"Popular sovereignty" is a political idea that says that people should be able to govern themselves by expressing their choices in votes.

Strong reaction

Congress voted on Douglas's bill in May 1854. It passed narrowly, by 115 votes to 104. There was an immediate backlash against the new act

Experts say that the Missouri Compromise could not have prevented violence forever.

among opponents of slavery. For 30 years, the Missouri Compromise had kept the balance between slave and free states. It said that no new states north of the 36° 30' line could be slave states. The new act destroyed that compromise. It potentially opened up Northern territory to slavery, if citizens voted in favor of it.

Political fallout

The act caused political uproar in the North. Douglas's Democratic Party, which was seen as representing Southern interests, took the blame. After the congressional elections in fall 1854, the number of northern Democrats in the House of Representatives fell from 92 to 23. On the other hand, more than 150 congressmen were elected on a platform of opposition to the act.

⟳ *A boy gets ready to fight a slave trader kicking slaves into Kansas.*

By 1856, opponents of the act had formed the Republican Party. The unpopularity of the act led to a Republican victory in the presidential elections of 1860. The election of Abraham Lincoln in turn led the Southern states to leave the Union... and so began the Civil War.

> The Republicans said that they would allow slavery to continue where it already existed, but not in new territory.

Bleeding Kansas

In Kansas, the act resulted in great violence. Some settlers were in favor of slavery, others were against it. Each attacked their opponents. There was so much bloodshed that the time was known as "Bleeding Kansas." Kansas was finally admitted to the Union as a free state in 1861.

> The violence and arguments continued in Kansas until the start of the Civil War in 1861.

THE RIGHT ANSWER

?

What was the importance of the Kansas–Nebraska Act in the path toward civil war?

The act created a situation in which settlers in a Northern territory would be able to choose to permit slavery. That would destroy the balance created by the Missouri Compromise of 1820. For 30 years, Northerners had been able to ignore the issue of slavery. The Kansas-Nebraska Act made it impossible to ignore it any more. The creation of the Republican Party and its victory in the 1860 presidential elections led directly to secession and to war. It also created one of the two great modern political parties of the United States.

Missouri Compromise

The Missouri Compromise of 1820 was the first political attempt to prevent conflict over slavery. It created a balance between free and slave states that lasted over 30 years.

⌒ **This group portrait marks a second compromise, in 1850.**

COMMENT

The Founders had largely ignored the issue of slavery. That left the problem for future politicians to solve.

Americans had always disagreed about slavery. When the United States was created, Southerners had demanded that each state should be able to decide for itself whether or not to permit slavery. The Founders agreed. The Southern states had all chosen to allow slavery; most Northern states had rejected it.

The problem remained of what should happen about slavery in any new states. That became more of an issue in the early 19th century, when the United States began to expand west. It became unavoidable in 1819, when the territory of Missouri applied for statehood.

Importance of Missouri

Congress had to pass a law to grant Missouri statehood. During the debate, Representative James Talmadge of New York suggested that any slaves in Missouri should be freed and that no others should be taken there. An intense debate began about whether the government had the power to restrict slavery in this way.

Some Northern congressmen supported Talmadge. They saw it as a first step in abolishing slavery altogether. But Southerners argued that they had a right to bring their property—including slaves—if they settled in the West.

The question was not just about rights, however. There was an equal number of free and slave states. That meant there was also an equal number of free-state and slave-state senators in the Senate. The addition of Missouri on either side would upset the political balance.

Slave owners saw slaves as pieces of property. Often, they were very valuable. If people lost a slave, they lost the money the slave had cost them.

A firebell in the night

The House of Representatives passed the bill, but Southerners blocked it in the Senate. When Congress debated it again in December 1819, Southerners had a new argument. They said that slavery was a "positive good." It helped slaves, masters, and the nation. Former president Thomas Jefferson wrote that the question of Missouri, "like a firebell in the night, awakened and filled me with terror."

⟳ *Henry Clay was a smart Kentucky politician. He was largely responsible for the Missouri Compromise.*

Details of the Compromise

To try to avoid civil war, Henry Clay, the Speaker of the House, came up with a compromise. He hoped that both Northerners and Southerners would support it. Clay suggested that Missouri would join the Union as a slave state. But another new state, Maine, would be created in northern Massachusetts. Maine would enter the Union as a free state. That way, the Senate would still have an even balance of power.

Jesse B. Thomas, an Illinois senator, added a suggestion to the compromise. He said that a line should be drawn on the map of the country along the southern border of Missouri (latitude 36° 30'). Any new states north of the line would be free; all states south of the line would be slave. All new states would enter the Union in pairs, one free and one slave. Clay was a smart politician, and he got the compromise passed. Missouri was admitted to the Union in March 1821.

Over the following 30 years, most Americans came to see the Missouri Compromise as being highly significant. It became treated as a sacred agreement between the North and South that would forever prevent a civil war over slavery.

> The Compromise worked because most politicians were not concerned with getting rid of slavery, but with keeping the balance of power.

↻ **This map shows the line on which the Missouri Compromise was based. Slave states could only exist south of the line.**

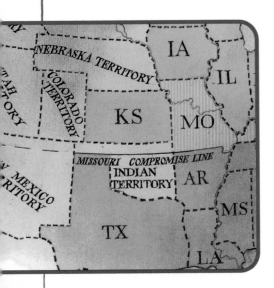

Recurring dispute

In the 1840s, the United States gained Texas, plus California and land in the Southwest from Spain. The issue of slavery in the territories arose again. A new compromise—the Compromise of 1850— again kept the Union together. But in 1854, the Kansas-Nebraska Act said that settlers could decide for themselves if territories would allow slavery, even in the North. That destroyed the Missouri Compromise. The time was near when no more compromises would be possible. The compromise over Missouri had kept the peace for decades. Now war was around the corner.

This new land mainly lay south of 36˚30', so was potentially open for slavery.

ASK YOURSELF

Would it have been better to preserve the Missouri Compromise than to allow settlers in new territories to decide whether or not to allow slavery?

THE RIGHT ANSWER

?

Could the Missouri Compromise have prevented a war over slavery forever?

In 1820, former president Thomas Jefferson had warned that the Missouri Compromise was only temporary. It was eventually destroyed by two major causes. First was the strength of feeling on both sides. Many Northerners were not just against the spread of slavery; they wanted all slavery abolished. Meanwhile, Southerners wanted their slaves treated as their legal property throughout the whole Union. Second, the United States kept expanding west. That meant that the question would not go away. Inevitably, the Compromise would one day fail to keep the peace.

Secession

When the United States was created, individual states chose to join it. Many Americans believed that states also had the right to choose to leave the Union. Leaving in this way is called secession.

In the first half of the 19th century, John C. Calhoun of South Carolina argued that a state could refuse to obey a federal law with which it disagreed. He also said that Southern states should secede if the U.S. Congress passed antislavery laws. After Calhoun died in 1850, other Southerners took up his cause.

In the second half of the 1850s, secession became more popular in the South. The new Republican Party in the North wanted to keep slavery out of the West. Secessionists argued that a Republican victory in the 1860 presidential election would justify secession.

⊍ *This engraving shows a meeting about secession in Charleston, South Carolina, in December 1860. South Carolina was the first state to leave the Union.*

Election of Lincoln

As soon as Abraham Lincoln was elected, South Carolina called a secession convention. The delegates voted to leave the Union on December 20, 1860, by a vote of 169 to 0. In January

1861, Mississippi, Florida, Alabama, Georgia, and Louisiana decided to secede. Texas became the seventh state to secede, on February 1. Representatives from the seceding states met to create the Confederate States of America.

Only the seven states of the Deep South had seceded. After the war began in April 1861, however, they were followed by four slave states of the Upper South: Virginia, Arkansas, North Carolina, and Tennessee. The secession of Virginia was particularly important: it was the most populous of the Southern states.

⋒ *Senator John C. Calhoun of South Carolina supported states' right to leave the Union.*

THE RIGHT ANSWER

?

Were states allowed to leave the Union under the terms of the U.S. Constitution?

The U.S. Constitution did not deal with the question of states wishing to leave the Union. It did not say that they could or that they could not. Therefore, both the Secessionists and their opponents could claim that the Constitution was on their side. Secessionists argued that ultimate authority still rested with the individual states. An agreement that had been voluntarily entered into could be voluntarily left. Unionists said that states that had entered the Union had chosen to accept the authority of the federal government and that they had to go on doing so.

Slavery

The institution of African slavery lay at the heart of the Civil War. It divided North from South in the United States. Few other issues would have led to a civil war between Americans.

⌐ **This engraving shows slaves working on a tobacco plantation in colonial America.**

Abraham Lincoln said in 1858 that the argument about slavery was simple. It was "between men who think slavery is wrong and those who do not." The debate was not new. The Spanish and Potuguese had slaves in their American colonies before the first European settlers arrived in North America in the early 17th century. As early as 1619, a year before the Pilgrims reached Plymouth, a shipment of West African slaves landed at Jamestown, Virginia. That first voyage began a trade that forcibly transported hundreds of thousands of Africans from their homelands to North America.

In the late 1700s, colonial Americans fought for their freedom from Britain in the name of liberty. But that liberty did not include slaves. Founders like George Washington and Thomas Jefferson owned large numbers of slaves. The U.S.

Constitution said that it was possible for one human being to own another.

By now, slavery was more widespread in some states than others. In South Carolina, slaves outnumbered the white population; New England had virtually no slaves. The split reflected an economic divide between the South and the North. The Southern states were suited to plantation agriculture, which relied on a large supply of cheap labor. The Northern states had much smaller, mixed farms. Such farms had little need for slavery.

The "peculiar institution"

The movement to abolish slavery began in Britain in the late 18th century. In 1807, Britain abolished the slave trade throughout its empire. The same year, the U.S. government also banned its Atlantic slave trade. By then, slavery had been banned or was being phased out in all the U.S. states north

ASK YOURSELF

What differences might it have made to the Constitution if the Founders had not owned slaves themselves?

Many of the leading protestors against slavery were Quakers. Their religion taught them that no one could have authority over anyone else.

⟲ A slave drives oxen pulling a cart loaded with baskets of cotton.

of Delaware. The nation was split between slave states and free states. More and more Northerners expressed their opposition to slavery.

Southerners called slavery the "peculiar institution." They meant that it only existed in the South, and that no one else understood it. Slavery supported a way of life very different from life in the North. Southerners said that slavery helped make life far more civilized than life in the Northern cities. They said that the slaves who sang in the cotton fields were happier than factory workers in the North.

↻ *Slaves process cotton in this drawing from the early 19th century.*

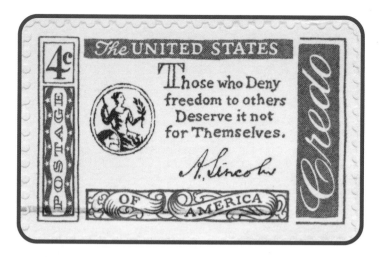

Myths of slavery

This view was contradicted by African Americans who had escaped from slavery. Former slaves such as Frederick Douglass described what slave life was really like. They recalled hardships such as being whipped or being separated from family members when one or another member was sold.

The rose-tinted view of slavery was even wrong about Southern whites. It was not accurate to suggest that Southern whites were a refined aristocracy. Only one in four Southerners owned any slaves. Most whites had to work for a living.

Not all slaves worked on large plantations. Slaves often worked alongside their masters on small farms. Slaves were also frequently hired out for various tasks, including skilled ones. Contracted-out slaves built railroads in the South. They could be found working together with free whites in the South's few factories, such as the Tredegar Ironworks in Richmond, Virginia.

One reason that slave owners did not want to educate their slaves was to make sure that they could not write true accounts of life in captivity.

ASK YOURSELF

Why might poor white Southerners support slavery, if they had no slaves themselves?

This painting from just after the Civil War shows an idealized view of agriculture in the South. Black slaves work happily as the planter and his wife look on.

ASK YOURSELF

Was it fair that slaves had no rights but could still be held responsible for their own actions?

Value of slavery

A huge amount of the wealth of the South was tied up in slavery. By 1860, there were nearly four million slaves (the total population of the South was nine million). A field hand was worth between $1,500 and $2,000. Many Southerners felt uneasy about slavery. But they could not imagine the economy without the slaves.

The legal situation of slaves was confused. On the one hand, a slave was legally defined as a piece of property, no different from a piece of furniture or a cow. On the other hand, slaves were also legally human beings. They were responsible for their own actions and could be tried for any crimes. This also meant that there were laws that set out to protect slaves from inhumane treatment.

Nature of slavery

The nature of slavery depended on the character of individual slave owners. Some were relatively kind. Others were cruel or harsh. Despite the laws, slaves were often mistreated. At its heart, slavery was based on force. Masters used their power to make a slave do their bidding; they used violence if it was necessary. The whole system relied on this threat of force. Without the threat, slaves either would not work or would simply move away. For many people in the North and beyond, the South's "peculiar institution" depended on a slave driver holding a whip.

Some owners provided good accommodation and food, and even taught their slaves to read and write.

ASK YOURSELF

Did slavery have to depend on violence? If all slave owners were kind, would that have made slavery more acceptable?

THE RIGHT ANSWER

?

Were Southerners right to defend slavery as a "peculiar institution"?

The idea of the "peculiar institution" was based on a belief that Northerners could not understand the role of slavery in the South. Southerners argued that the slave economy allowed wealthy whites to live in a way that was morally superior to life in the industrial cities of the North. They also said that the system helped slaves, by teaching them Christianity and providing them with a carefree existence. But the Southern argument broke down because of the obvious hardships of slave life and because the institution ultimately relied on force and violence to preserve it.

States' Rights

Many Americans, particularly in the South, believed that the Constitution gave states some rights to govern themselves. The federal government of the United States could not change these powers.

W hen the Southern states left the Union in 1861, they said that secession was necessary to prevent the federal government interfering with the rights of individual states. But states' rights were closely linked to slavery: the most important right for the Southern states was the right to keep slaves.

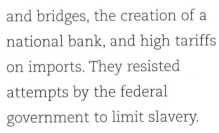

⟲ *Citizens meet in Savannah, Georgia, on November 8, 1860. They called for Georgia to leave the Union.*

History of states' rights

The debate over states' rights was as old as the United States. Supporters of states' rights tended to oppose federal aid for projects such as roads and bridges, the creation of a national bank, and high tariffs on imports. They resisted attempts by the federal government to limit slavery.

The Constitution had left almost all matters regarding slavery in the hands of the states. But it was less clear about whether slavery should be allowed in new territories. Southerners thought that the property rights in the Constitution gave them the right to take their slave property anywhere, including the new territories.

When Republican Abraham Lincoln was elected president in 1860, the first seven states seceded before he took office. Most secessionists used a states' rights argument. They argued that since the individual states had voluntarily joined the Union, they now had the right to leave it.

🎧 *Parts of the North were very industrial. Southerners said that Northerners were only interested in making money.*

THE RIGHT ANSWER

?

Was the secession of the South really about states' rights, or was it about slavery?

Confederate leaders said that they seceded to defend states' rights. That appealed to countries like Britain and France, which would not support a campaign to defend slavery. It also appealed to the majority of Southern whites, who owned no slaves and would not necessarily fight for the rights of rich men to own slaves. After the war, as more Americans came to see slavery as inhumane, Southerners increasingly argued that the war was really about states' rights. In fact, the only states' right most Southerners cared about enough to fight for was the right to keep slavery.

Uncle Tom's Cabin

Uncle Tom's Cabin was one of the most influential novels ever written. Published in 1852, it was a story about slavery. For many Americans, it was a shocking revelation of the horrors of slave life.

⌓ *An illustration from the book shows Tom being sold at a slave auction.*

The book was written by Harriet Beecher Stowe. She was born in Connecticut in 1811. Her family was very religious and also believed that girls should have an education.

When she grew up, Harriet worked as a teacher. She also wrote stories for Christian publications. In 1836, she married Calvin E. Stowe, a professor of theology.

In 1850, Harriet and her family moved to Maine. That same year, Congress passed the Fugitive Slave Law. The law said that slave owners could hunt for runaway slaves anywhere in the country, even in free states. It also said that the public had a duty to help catch the runaways, even if they were opposed to slavery.

Like many Northerners, Harriet was furious about the new law. She started writing *Uncle Tom's*

Cabin as her response. It told the story of Tom, a slave, and his three owners. Each owner is different: One is kind, for example, but another is violent and cruel. The story showed how slavery destroyed families and brought suffering to individuals.

After appearing in a magazine, *Uncle Tom's Cabin* was published in book form in 1852. It sold 50,000 copies in eight weeks. It was the bestselling novel of the 19th century. Readers were fascinated to learn about the horrors of slavery. It was so influential that some people think it helped start the Civil War.

⊙ *Harriet Beecher Stowe said about* Uncle Tom's Cabin, *"God wrote the book. I took his dictation."*

THE RIGHT ANSWER

?

Did *Uncle Tom's Cabin* play an important role in the causes of the Civil War?

For many readers outside the South, the novel's description of how slaves really lived was very uncomfortable. It forced them to think about the morality of slavery. It helped convince more people that slavery was an evil that had to be ended. The actual causes of the war were more about political and economic power in the United States. But Harriet's novel had helped strengthen antislavery feelings in the North and made it more difficult for slavery to be ignored. President Abraham Lincoln called her "the little lady who wrote the book that made this great war."

Underground Railroad

The Underground Railroad helped slaves escape from the South. Volunteers took the runaways to the North or Canada. The journey was difficult. There was a constant threat of capture.

↻ Runaway slaves shoot at the slave hunters who are chasing them.

The Underground Railroad was a network of secret routes set up by antislavery groups in the North. There were safe houses along the way where slaves could stay. From the 1830s, volunteers disguised as peddlers headed south to tell slaves about the network. When runaways reached the North, "conductors" would guide them along the route.

There was no organization to aid runaway slaves, but some individuals provided help. Abolitionists also formed urban vigilance committees to help runaways. Those committees were busiest after the Fugitive Slave Act was passed in 1850. The law meant that runaways could be returned to their owners at any time.

A few daring activists ventured into the South to free slaves. The best known rescuer was Harriet Tubman. She freed as many as 300 slaves.

Escape

By 1860, some 100,000 slaves had escaped on the Underground Railroad. Most were not just "passengers," however. They actively planned their own escapes. Many runaways traveled on foot at night. They stole food from farms and hid from slave hunters in hedgerows or barns. Others traveled by boat as stowaways or illegal passengers. One man even mailed himself to the North in a large crate.

‹ *A group of fugitive slaves makes their way north through a rainstorm.*

COMMENT

Henry Brown shipped himself from Virginia to Philadelphia in a wooden crate in 1849. The journey took 27 hours.

THE RIGHT ANSWER

?

How good was the Underground Railroad at rescuing people from slavery?

Especially after the war, the Underground Railroad was often described as a highly popular organization whose many supporters helped many thousands of slaves to freedom. The reality was more limited. Many people in the North were hostile to abolition, and safe houses were few and far between. In addition, slaves could only join the Underground Railroad after they had already reached the North. In reality, it was the slaves who took most risks, not the "conductors." Most slaves had to plan their own escape and travel across the South.

Glossary

abolition: Making slavery illegal; supporters of abolition were called abolitionists.

compromise: A solution to a problem that avoids extremes so that both sides can agree on it.

Confederacy: The word used to describe the Southern side in the Civil War; it refers to a group of equal members with a common purpose.

convention: A political meeting that considers a specific question.

electoral college: A body of people who represent the voters in each state and elect the president and vice president.

federal: Related to the U.S. government in Washington, D.C.

fugitive: Someone who has escaped and is in hiding from the police or other authorities.

house slave: A slave who did tasks in their owner's home.

martyr: Someone who willingly dies for a particular cause.

"peculiar institution": A term used by people in the South to suggest that only Southerners could understand the real nature of slavery.

plantation: A large-scale agricultural estate that was used to grow crops such as sugar, tobacco, and cotton.

Quaker: A Christian who belongs to the Society of Friends.

radical: Someone who holds extreme views.

secession: Breaking away from the Union.

sovereignty: The ability of a group of people to govern themselves.

territory: An area of the United States where settlers lived, but which was not organized enough to become a state.

Union: The Northern side in the Civil War—the United States of America.

Further reading

Carlson, Julie. *Uncle Tom's Cabin and the Abolitionist Movement.* (Looking at Literature through Primary Sources). Rosen Publishing Group, 2004.

Koestler-Grack, Rachel. *Abraham Lincoln.* (Leaders of the Civil War Era). Chelsea House Publishers, 2009.

Lassieur, Allison. *The Underground Railroad: An Interactive History Adventure*. Capstone Press, 2008.

McNeese, Tim. *Dred Scott v. Sandford: The Pursuit of Freedom* (Great Supreme Court Decisions). Chelsea House Publications, 2006.

Miller, Reagan. *A Nation Divided: Causes of the Civil War*. (Understanding the Civil War). Crabtree Publishing Company, 2011.

Mountjoy, Shane. *Causes of the Civil War: The Differences Between the North and the South.* Chelsea House Publishers, 2009.

Wagner, Heather Lehr. *The Outbreak of the Civil War: A Nation Tears Apart*. Chelsea House, 2009.

Websites

History Place interactive timeline of the Civil War.
http//www.historyplace.com/civilwar

Smithsonian Institution page with resources on the Civil War.
http//www.civilwar.si.edu

The gateway page to the National Archives pages about the Atlantic slave trade and its abolition.
http://www.nationalarchives.gov.uk/slavery/

A site supporting the famed PBS film *The Civil War*, directed by Ken Burns.
http//www.pbs.org/civilwar

Publisher's note to educators and parents: Our editors have carefully reviewed these websites to ensure that they are suitable for students. Many websites change frequently, however, and we cannot guarantee that a site's future contents will continue to meet our high standards of quality and educational value. Be advised that students should be closely supervised whenever they access the Internet.

Index